SMART BRAIN RIGHT BRAIN

An Introduction to Mechanical Engineering

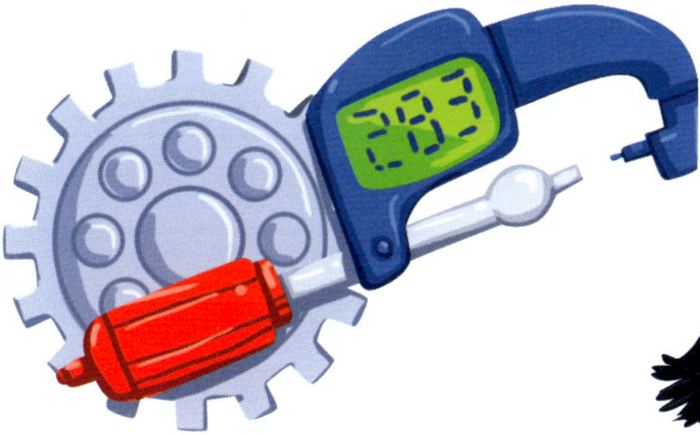

Om KIDZ
An imprint of Om Books International

First Published in 2021 by

Om Kidz | Om Books International

Corporate & Editorial Office
A-12, Sector 64, Noida 201 301
Uttar Pradesh, India
Phone: +91 120 477 4100
Email: editorial@ombooks.com
Website: www.ombooksinternational.com

Sales Office
107, Ansari Road, Darya Ganj
New Delhi 110 002, India
Phone: +91 11 4000 9000
Email: sales@ombooks.com

Author: Shweta Sinha
Editor: Kirti Pathak
Art & Design: Anshuman Pandey, Gaurav Bhandari, Harish Arya

ISBN: 978-93-5276-846-2

Printed in India

10 9 8 7 6 5 4 3 2 1

CONTENTS

1. Machines, Force and Energy

All machines need a force to work. You **push** down the pedals to move your bicycle. You **pull** the handles of a pair of scissors together to cut paper.

To generate the force, energy is needed. Energy is the ability to do work. Your body generates energy from the food you eat. Similarly, here are some other sources of energy:

Most vehicles run on fossil fuels. Petrol, diesel and natural gas are types of fossil fuels. Fossil fuels have **chemical** energy.

Household appliances often require **electrical** energy. We even have electric cars, buses and trains.

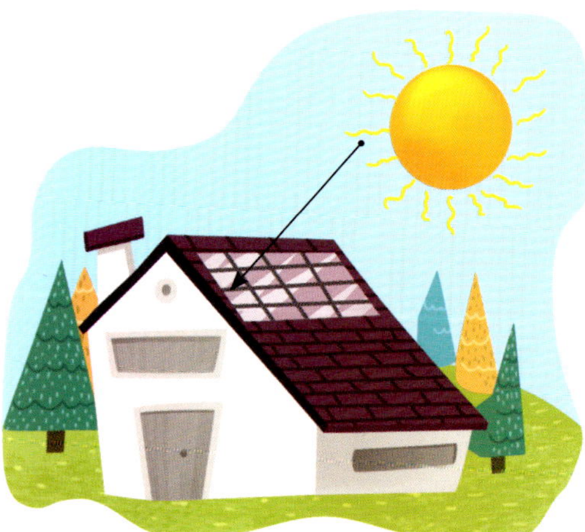

You may have seen solar panels fitted on rooftops. These panels use the Sun's energy or **solar** energy to generate electricity.

Wind energy pushes the sails of a sailboat forward and turns a windmill around.

We also use wind energy and energy from moving water, like rivers and tides, to generate electricity.

Water Energy

Wind Energy

DID YOU KNOW?

Fossil fuel is a non-renewable energy source. One day we will use up all of Earth's fossil fuel reserves.

2. Pedal Power

A bicycle is the coolest machine that you can use for getting around. It uses many simple machines. A bicycle does not need an engine to work. All you need are the pedals. Pedals are connected to cranks, which in turn are connected to the back wheel by a chain. When you push the pedals up and down, it turns the cranks round and round, thus powering the wheel.

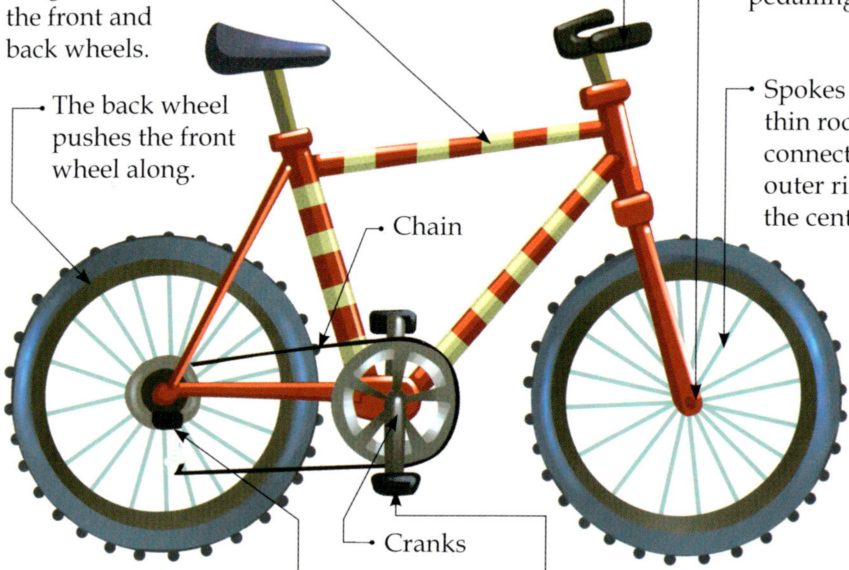

POCKET FACT

We use muscular force to run a bicycle.

Slower or faster?

Gears are wheels with teeth, called cogs. Two gears link up the chain on a bicycle. They make pedalling easy and fast.

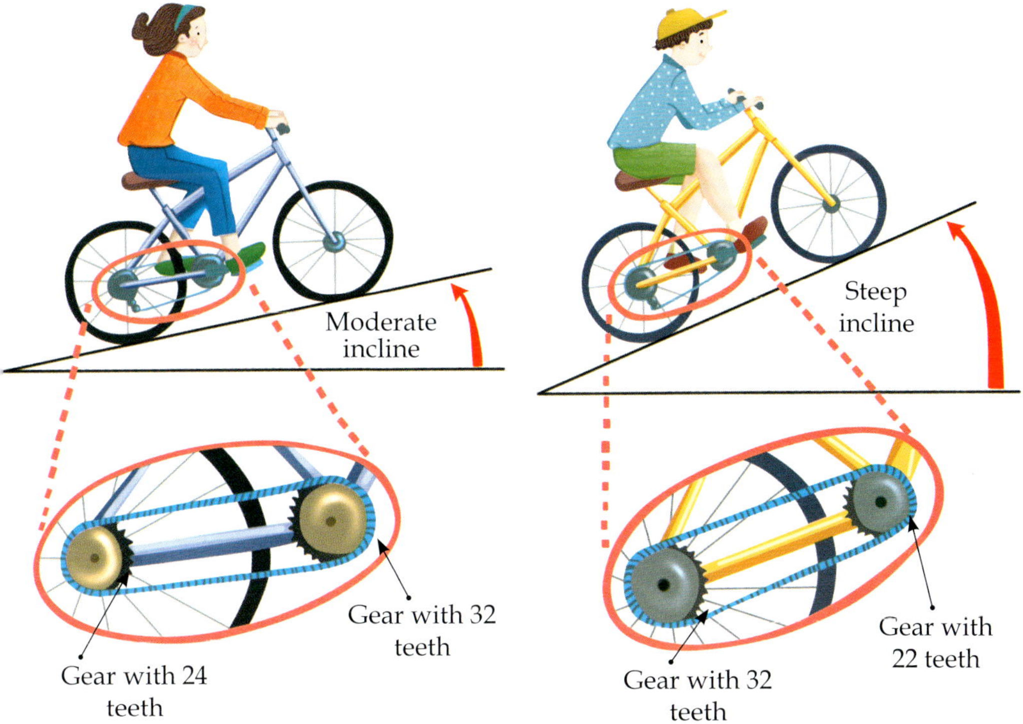

Larger gear at the front, connected to a smaller gear at the back keeps the bicycle in high gear. This setting helps you speed up on level ground or when going downhill.

Smaller gear at the front, connected to a larger gear at the back keeps the bicycle in low gear. This is best suited for cycling uphill.

DID YOU KNOW?

A bicycle is so efficient it can convert up to 90 percent of your pedalling energy into forward motion of the wheels.

Types of bicycles

Utility bicycles are designed for everyday use. The focus is on riding comfort. Chain guards prevent the oily chains from staining clothes. Some have front baskets to carry stuff.

Mountain bicycles have wider tyres for a better grip on uneven terrain. The frame and the wheel spokes are stronger to handle the rough riding.

Racing bicycles are made for speed, not endurance. They have lightweight frames, thin tyres and no brakes. Drop handlebars allow the rider to bend low and make a streamlined shape to ride faster.

Holding the road

The tyres on the wheels are not smooth. They have patterns called **treads** that help them get a good grip on the road surface, even when it is rainy. This makes it easy for you to control the bicycle.

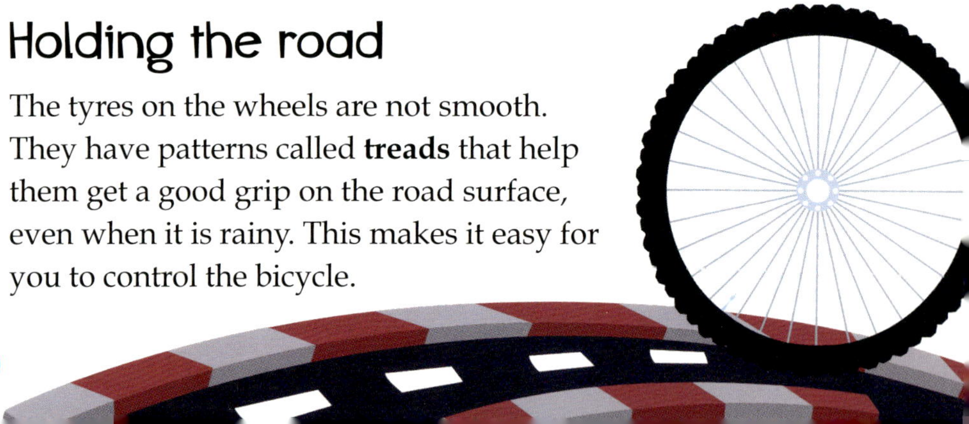

3. Travel Machines

Unlike a bicycle, a car has an engine under its hood. A car engine is a machine that burns fuel to generate mechanical energy. Fuels such as petrol and diesel require only a small spark to catch fire. The engine is powered by a series of small fires. At normal speed, a car's engine triggers nearly 50 fires per second.

Basic components of a car

Sun roof
Car windows are made of a special glass that doesn't shatter easily.

Exhaust Pipe
Releases the car's emissions from the burning fuel.

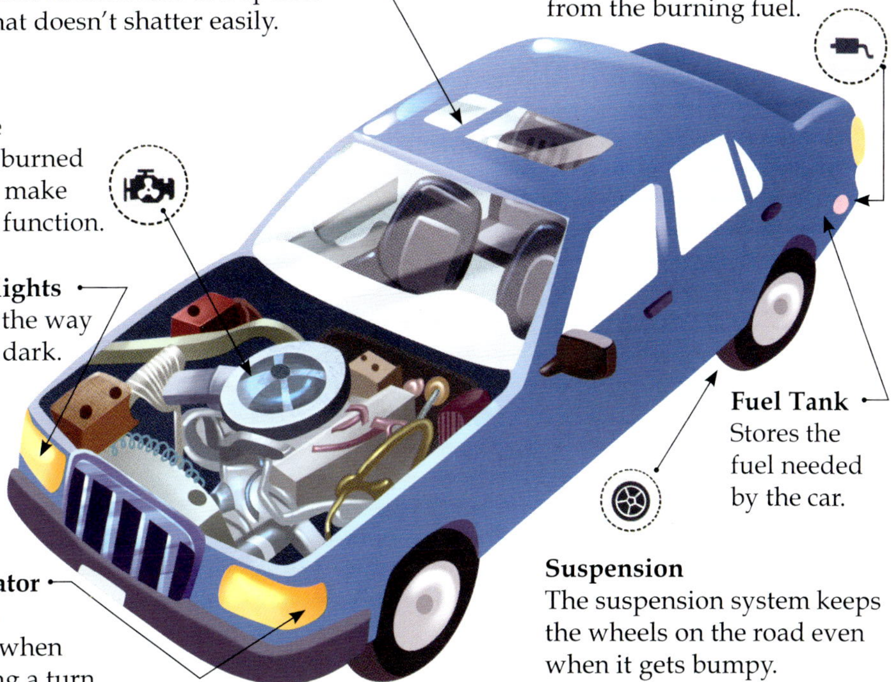

Engine
Fuel is burned here to make the car function.

Headlights
Show the way in the dark.

Fuel Tank
Stores the fuel needed by the car.

Indicator lights
Used when making a turn.

Suspension
The suspension system keeps the wheels on the road even when it gets bumpy.

POCKET FACT To make a fire, all you need is fuel, oxygen in the air and a spark.

How does a car move?

So how does the car engine turn the wheels? It's not much different from how you ride a bicycle. If you look inside a car engine, you will find that it is made up of cylinder-shaped cooking pots. Each cylinder has pistons that move up and down, just like your legs do when you ride a bicycle.

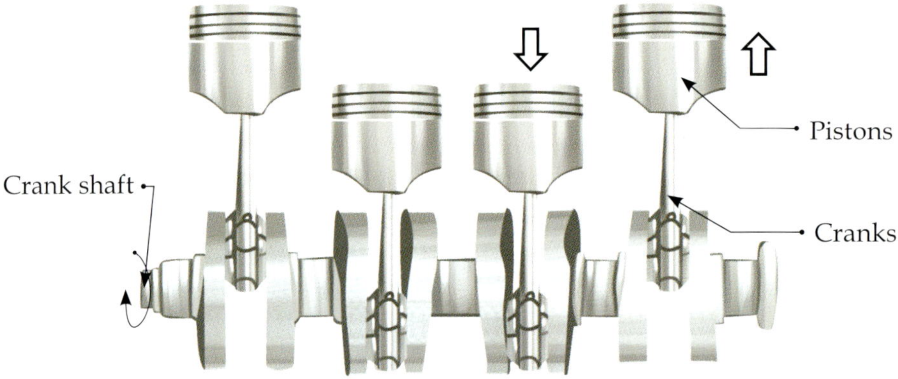

Pistons are connected to levers called cranks. The pistons turn the cranks round and round.

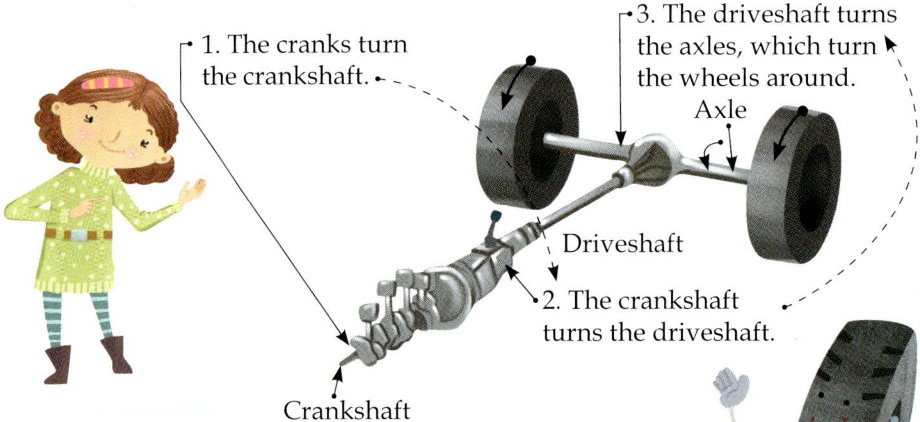

DID YOU KNOW?

Car wheels come with air-filled tyres that bend with the bumps on the road. A brand new car wheel called a **tweel** has flexible spokes instead of rubber tyres.

On the go

Vehicles come in different shapes and sizes and are used for different purposes.

- A **motorcycle** has two wheels like a bicycle. It is designed to seat two people.
- A **car** typically has four wheels and can carry a small number of people.
- A **race car** is like a normal car in most ways. However, it is built to run fast with a lighter, smoother body. It has a powerful engine with eight cylinders.
- A **tractor** has a powerful engine too, but for carrying heavy loads and not for speed. Its big, wide wheels with deep treads provide a better grip on muddy and slimy surfaces.
- A **bus** is a large road vehicle designed to carry a large number of people. Some buses can carry as many as 300 passengers.
- A **truck** is used to transport cargo. Trucks can vary in size and capacity. Smaller pickup trucks are similar to cars. Larger trucks are powered by diesel engines capable of carrying heavy loads. Some trucks are fitted with equipment for specialised purposes such as fire trucks and concrete mixers.

Car or truck?

When you put the body of a pickup truck on a bus axle with tractor wheels, this is what you get - a **Monster Truck**. The raised body lets it jump over almost any large obstacle.

4. Trains on Tracks

Most countries have a rail transport system where trains run on tracks. A railroad track is made of two steel rails placed at the same fixed distance from each other. This fixed distance is called the **gauge**. The two rails are connected to each other with sleepers made of wood or concrete.

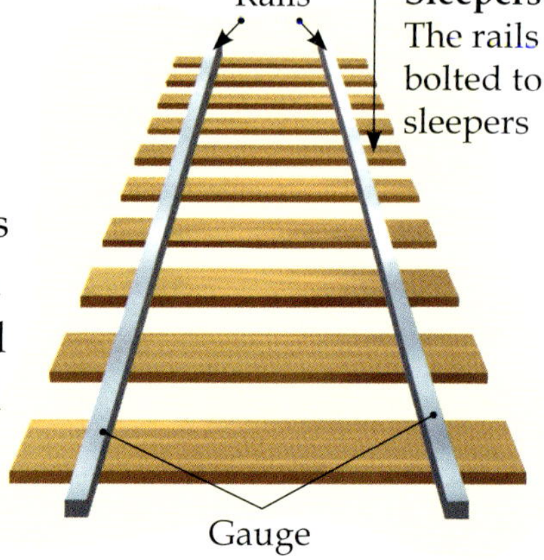

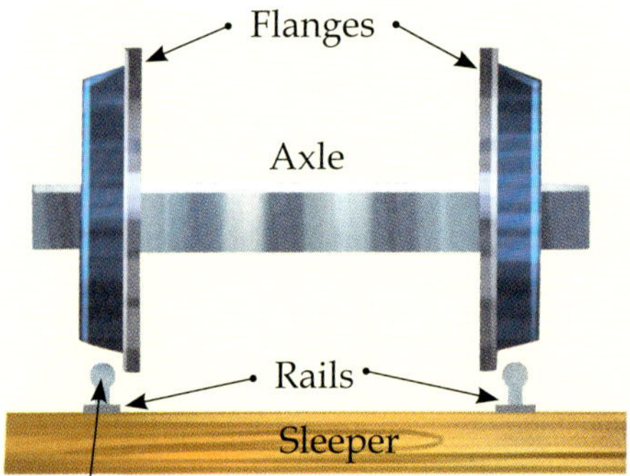

The wheels of a train are made of steel too and are specially designed to grip the tracks. The wheels are slightly cone-shaped, with the wider side on the inside. They have metal rims called **flanges** that keep them from slipping off the tracks. The two wheels are connected to a straight axle, ensuring that both wheels rotate together.

Mountain Rails

When running up steep slopes, trains have to go really slow or risk slipping down the tracks. To overcome this problem, trains are fitted with cog wheels. Cogs are wheels with teeth. They mesh into a rack system that runs in the middle of the rail tracks. This helps the train get a better grip on the track and reach much higher speeds.

Full steam ahead

Like cars, the job of a rail engine or a locomotive is to convert energy into motion. Different types of locomotives are powered in different ways.

Steam Locomotive

The first trains were pulled by steam locomotives. These engines burnt coal to boil water into steam that powered them. Today you can find steam locomotives in museums and are not in use anymore.

Diesel-Electric

These engines burn diesel fuel to generate electricity. The electricity is then used to power the locomotive and move the wheels forward.

Electric Engine

An electric engine runs on electricity that is supplied through a third rail. The train has a device called a shoe to pick up the electric current.

Another type of electric locomotive picks up electricity from overhead cables using a metal arm called pantograph.

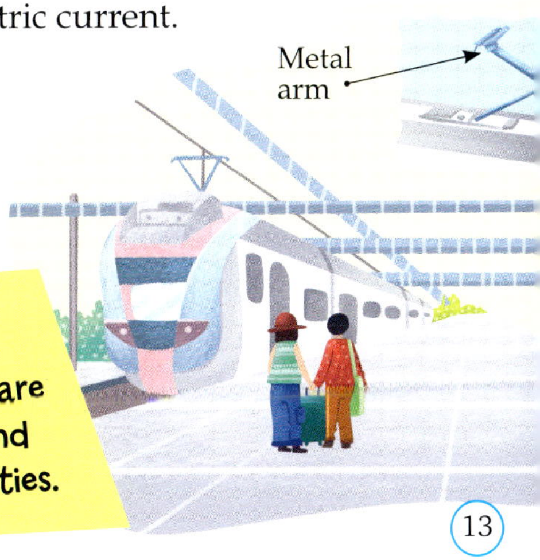

POCKET FACT

Some trains use combined engines that are powered by electricity in urban areas and use a diesel engine in terrains outside cities.

5. Floating and Flying

Ships are massive travel machines. They are heavy, especially when full of passengers, crew and cargo. Yet they are able to float on water.

What keeps a ship afloat?

'Buoyancy' is what keeps ships and boats floating on water. When an object is dropped in a liquid, it displaces a certain amount of liquid. If the object weighs lesser than the weight of the liquid displaced, the object will float. But if the object is heavier, it sinks.

Two forces act on a ship. While **gravity** pulls it downwards, **buoyancy** pushes it upwards. These forces balance each other out, letting the ship float.

A ship can sink if it springs a leak and takes in water. Bulkheads are walls that divide large areas onto smaller compartments. If one section starts a leak, the bulkhead prevents water from flooding the entire ship.

DID YOU KNOW?

A submarine needs to both sink or float on command. They achieve this by filling or emptying their ballast tanks with air or water.

How do planes fly?

Aerodynamics means the movement of air. Four aerodynamic forces work on an aeroplane in flight. An aeroplane needs to balance all these forces to fly.

Thrust moves the plane forward. A plane needs to create enough thrust to balance out the drag. The propellers create the thrust by sucking in air past the blades.

Lift is the force opposite to the weight. Lift is created by the wings.

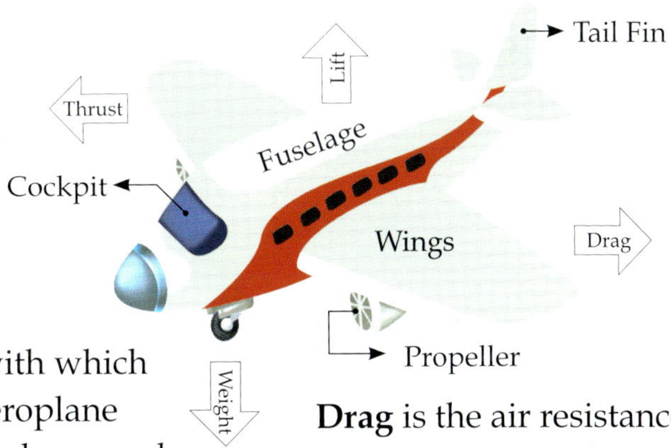

Weight is the force with which the Earth pulls the aeroplane downwards. An aeroplane needs to create a lot of lift to overcome its weight.

Drag is the air resistance that slows down the plane. It works opposite to the thrust. A plane's streamlined body is designed to reduce drag.

Lift Off!

The wings of an aeroplane are designed in such a way that it creates the lift. Wind flows both over and under the wings of an aeroplane. The top of the wing is curved, making air flow faster above the wing than under it. The slow moving air under the wings pushes the aeroplane upwards. This creates the 'lift'.

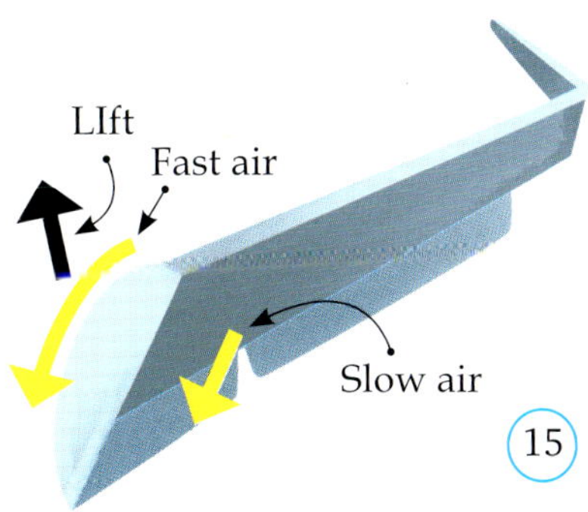

6. Big Machines

Shifting loads, digging dirt, lifting hefty objects - machines at a construction site need to do a lot of heavy work. The science behind these big machines is fairly simple.

Bulldozers are powerful heavy equipment used during construction or demolition.

A long claw-like device at the back of the bulldozer, is used to loosen debris, making it easy to handle. This device is called a 'ripper'.

Wide tracks distribute the bulldozer's weight over a large area. This lets them easily drive over uneven, muddy or sandy ground.

The heavy metal blade in the front is the bulldozer's primary tool. It is used for pushing large amounts of rubble or dirt.

A **digger** is used to scoop up rubble and dig into the ground. It has a set of connected levers that are joined like the parts of a human arm.

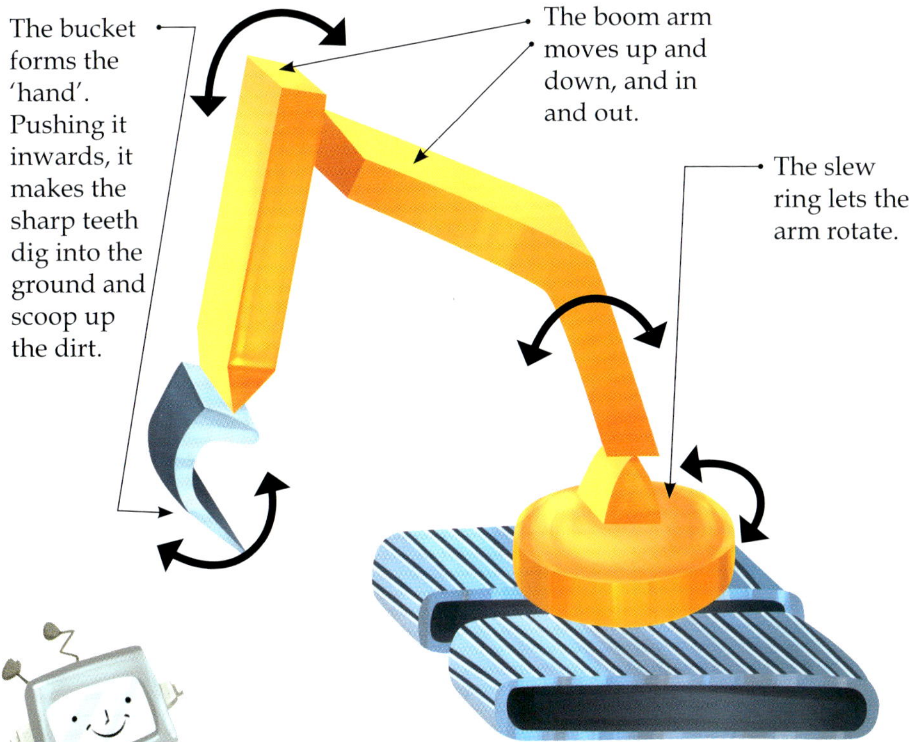

DID YOU KNOW?

An **excavator** is another name for a digger.

Tower Crane

Tower cranes help construct tall buildings.

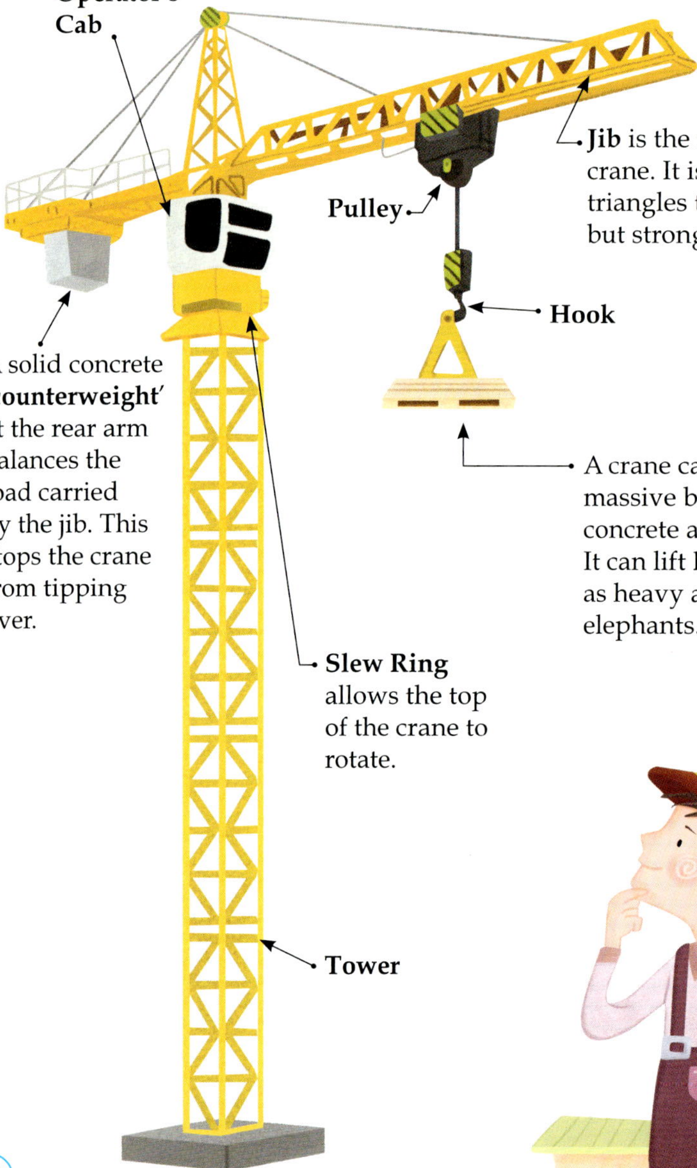

Other Movers and Shakers

A **concrete mixer** mixes together the ingredients that make concrete - usually gravel, water and cement. It keeps the mixture sloshing inside in liquid form until ready to pour.

A **dump truck** has a deep open bed at the rear that can be filled with sand, gravel or demolition waste to be transported.

A **mobile crane** is used for smaller jobs.

DID YOU KNOW?

The first thing that a tower crane does when it arrives at a construction site is to build itself.

7. Everyday Machines

You use many machines everyday without even realising it. The clock on the wall, the lawnmower, and the ballpoint pen you write with, are all machines.

A **mechanical clock** tells time using gears, a pendulum and a mainspring. A pendulum is a weight that hangs from a string.

As the pendulum swings, the weight always takes the same amount of time to swing out from its starting point and back again. This regular movement ensures that the gears move at the right pace and the clock keeps time accurately.

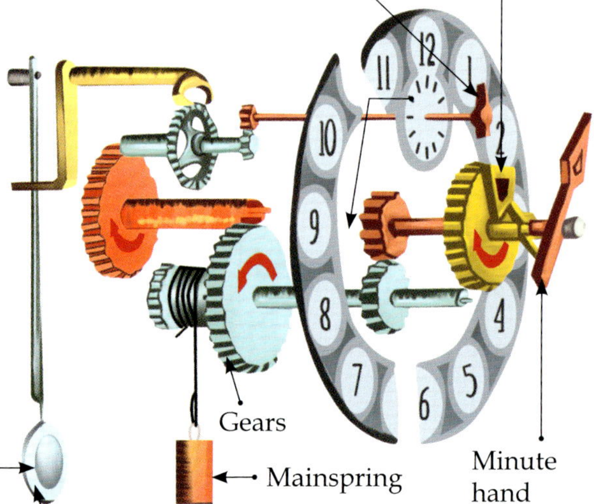

The clock is wound with a key that tightens the mainspring. As the mainspring unwinds, it turns the gears which then move the hands of the clock.

A **lawnmower** has an engine like that of a car. However, the engine is much smaller and has only one cylinder. This means there is only one piston going up and down to move the mower's wheels.

Do you enjoy going click-click-click on a retractable **ballpoint pen**? The pen has levers inside that push out the pen tip when you press the button. When you press it again, the lever gets released and the pen tip retracts into the pen cavity.

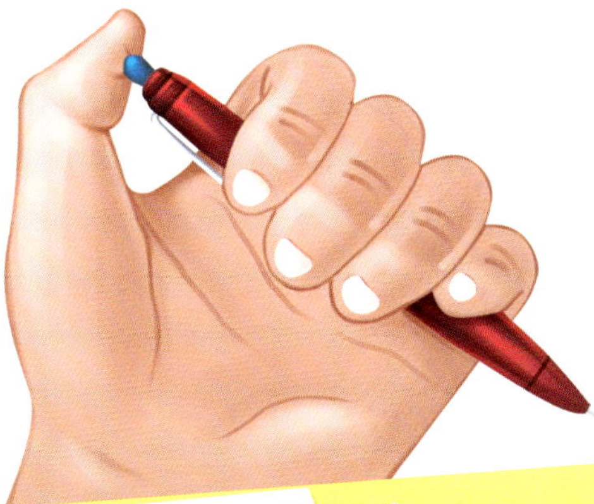

POCKET FACT

A quartz clock uses gears like a mechanical clock, but has quartz crystals instead of a pendulum. All quartz crystals vibrate at the same frequency and help keep time.

Lock it up

A **padlock** requires a **key** to unlock it. Every key has a unique profile of ridges and raised areas. So, a key will only open the lock it is meant for.

The working of a lock

If you look inside a lock, you will find a metal housing containing a cylinder. A series of thin metal pins drop from the housing into the cylinder, locking the cylinder in place. To open the lock, the key must free the cylinder from the pins and rotate it.

Inside a lock

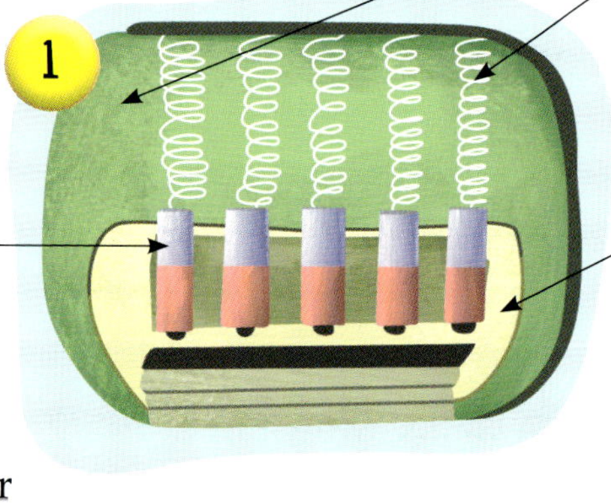

When a key is inserted, it pushes the pins against the force of the springs. If the wrong key is inserted, all pins are not pushed up correctly and the cylinder remains locked.

2

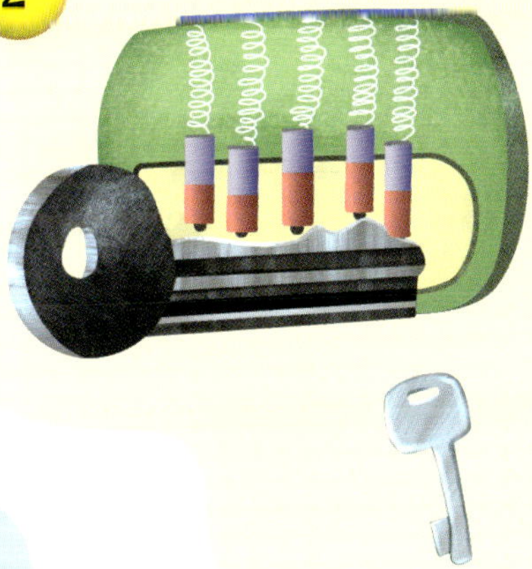

3

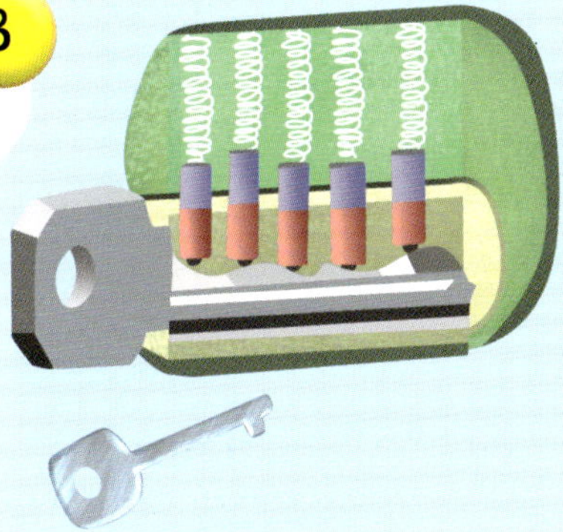

With the correct key all the upper set of pins are pushed above the cylinder.

4

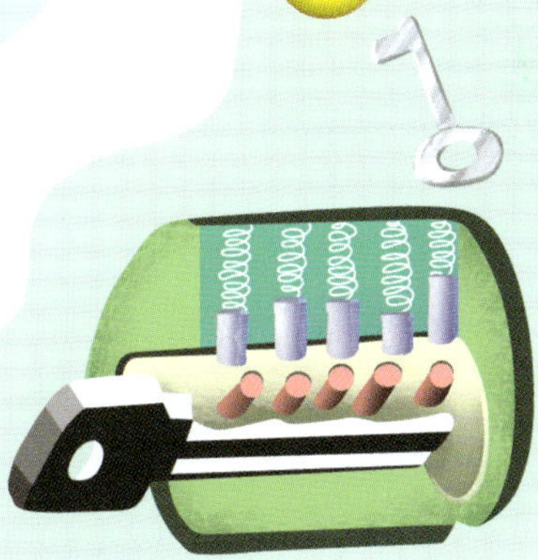

Now the cylinder is free to rotate. When you turn the key, it opens the lock.

DID YOU KNOW?

A combination lock opens with a secret combination of numbers. This lock has a wheel pack with one wheel for each number in the combination.

8. Activity: Let's Make A Toy Car

Have you played around with a rubber band, stretching it with your fingers and then letting it go flying? A rubber band can help you launch a simple toy car and also be a fun way to learn about machines.

You need:

- A small, sturdy cardboard box
- Two unsharpened pencils
- Rubber bands
- Scissors
- Glue

Step 1. Cut the cardboard box in half. Tape any loose flaps securely on all sides.

Step 2. Poke two holes in the front of the box for wheels. The holes should be aligned in a straight line. They should be larger than the pencils for a pencil to turn freely. Poke holes in the rear of the box similarly.

Step 3. Insert pencils through the holes to make sure they turn freely.

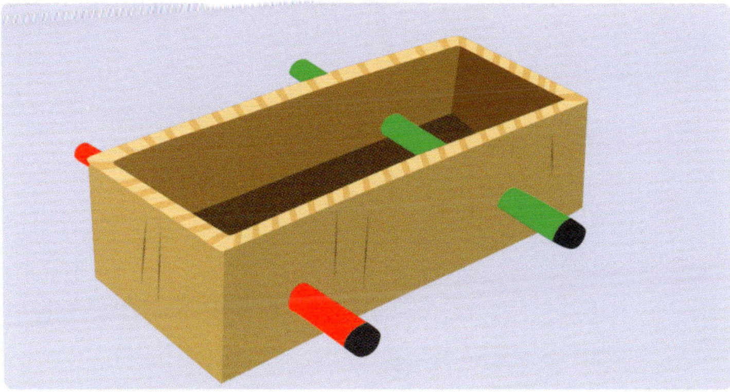

Step 4. Cut out two 'V-shaped' notches in the front of the box. Keep the square in the middle fairly large. It has to be strong enough to support the rubber band.

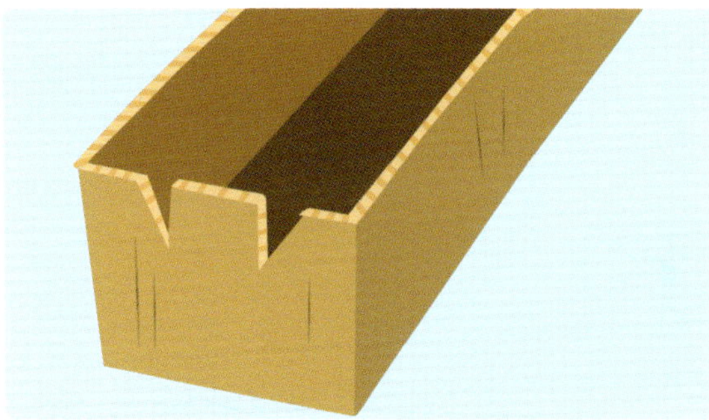

Step 5. Use the remaining part of the box to cut out four cardboard wheels. Bigger wheels help the car travel a longer distance. Make a hole in the centre of each wheel. The hole should be just right to fix a pencil and not larger.

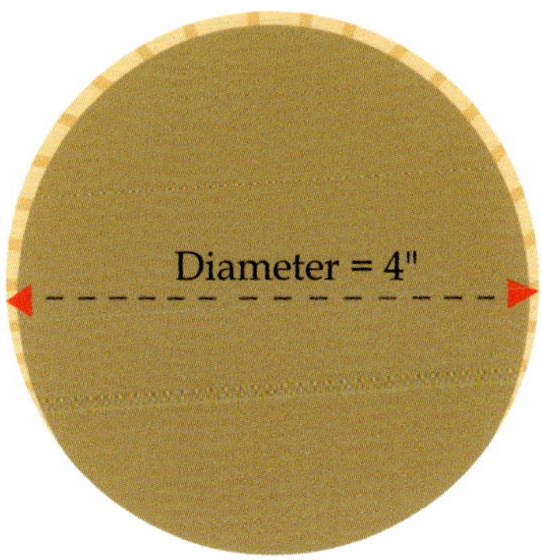

Step 6. Fix a wheel on one pencil and push it through the holes in the back of the car. The pencil forms the axle of the wheel assembly.

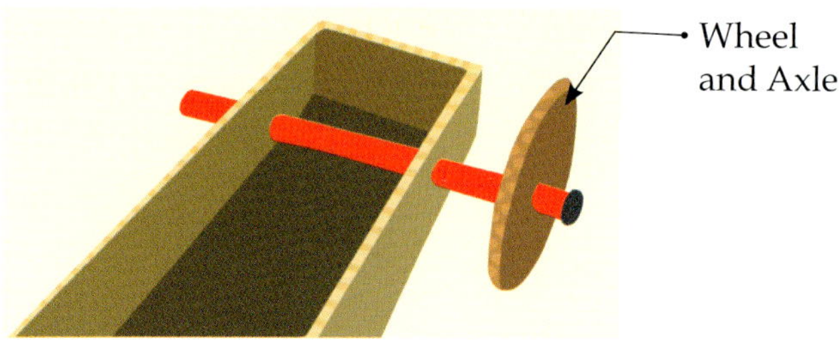

Step 7. Fix another wheel to the other end of the pencil. Apply some glue on the pencils near the hole in the cardboard wheels. Slide the wheels over the glue until they stick securely to the pencils. Repeat the steps for the front wheel assembly.

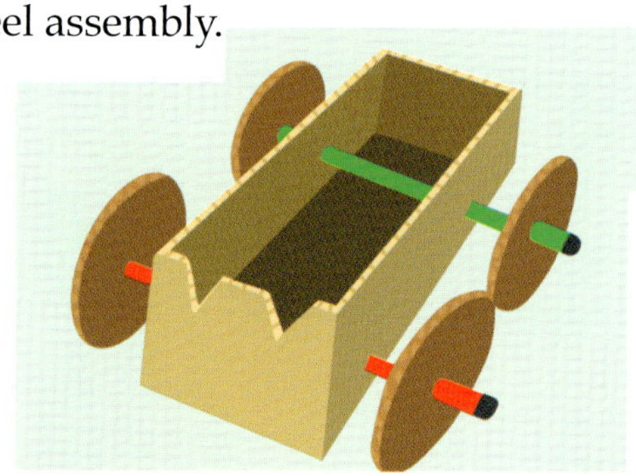

Step 8. Depending on the length of your car, join together one or more rubber bands. The length should be a bit smaller than the distance between the notches in the front and the rear pencil. Loop one end on the notches.

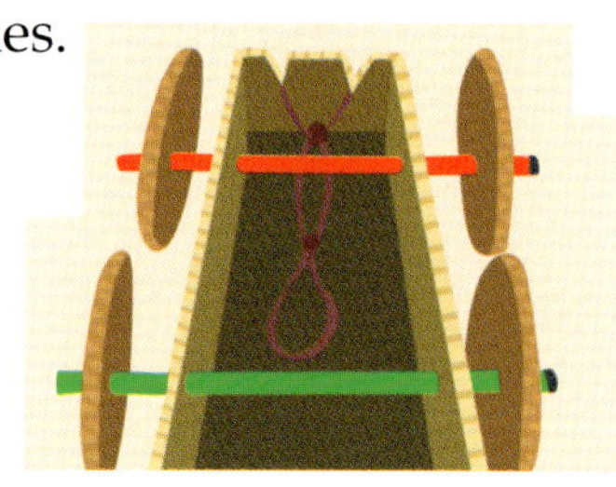

Step 9. Your toy car is now ready. Make sure it can roll smoothly. Place it on a flat surface and give it a small push. You may need to adjust the wheels so they do not wobble.

Launching your car

Hold the rear pencil with your fingers. Pull the open end of the rubber band to the rear pencil and turn the pencil to wind the band around it. After a couple of turns you can feel the rubber band pulling on the pencil. Place the car on the floor and release the pencil. Watch your car take off! How far did it go?

What happened?

You have read that all machines need energy to do work. In this case, the source of energy is the rubber band.

When the rubber band is wound around the rear axle, you store something known as **potential energy**. The rubber band is not yet doing anything, but the energy it holds has the 'potential' to do something.

When you release the pencil, the rubber band begins to unwind. The potential energy gets converted into kinetic energy. **Kinetic energy** is the energy of motion. It propels your car forward.

POCKET FACT

Potential energy is also called the 'energy at rest' as this form of energy remains stored until it is used up to produce an action or motion.

Let's Get Active

Crossword Puzzle

Across:

1. The energy of motion.

6. Patterns on a tyre are called __________.

9. Wheels with teeth.

10. Thrust, lift, drag and weight are _______ forces that an aeroplane needs to balance.

11. These powerful equipments are used during construction or demolition.

12. This machine has an engine like a car with only one cylinder.

Down:

2. The ability to do work.

3. A combination lock opens with a secret combination of __________.

4. Type of force that runs a bicycle.

5. Walls that divide large areas onto smaller compartments in ships.

7. This ship can both sink or float on command.

8. A _____________ is a weight that hangs from a string. It helps clocks keep time.

Jumbled Words

Unscramble the words to find the right machine for the job.

A machine you will choose if you...

1. were constructing a tall building.	ERTWO RNECA
2. needed to keep your house safe from burglars.	CKOLS
3. had to travel quickly between two far-off cities.	EEAANORLP
4. wanted to sign a document.	ABILLNOPT ENP
5. needed to transport a large amount of cargo across the country.	AINRT
6. were digging a large hole in the ground.	GGDEIR

Test your machine knowledge

Choose the best option to complete the sentence:

1. The ______ in a car engine move up and down and turn the ______ round and round.

   (a) pedals, cranks

   (b) cranks, crankshaft

   (c) pistons, cranks

2. A cycle is in ______ gear when it has a larger gear at the front, connected to a smaller gear at the back.

   (a) high

   (b) medium

   (c) low

3. A monster truck has the body of a ______, the axles of a ______ and the wheels of a ______.

   (a) bus, pickup truck, car

   (b) car, bus, train

   (c) pickup truck, bus, tractor

4. The fixed distance between the two steel rails in a railroad track is called ______.

   (a) length

   (b) gauge

   (c) measure

5. ______ keeps the ships floating on water.

   (a) Lift

   (b) Buoyancy

   (c) Drag

Label the Machine

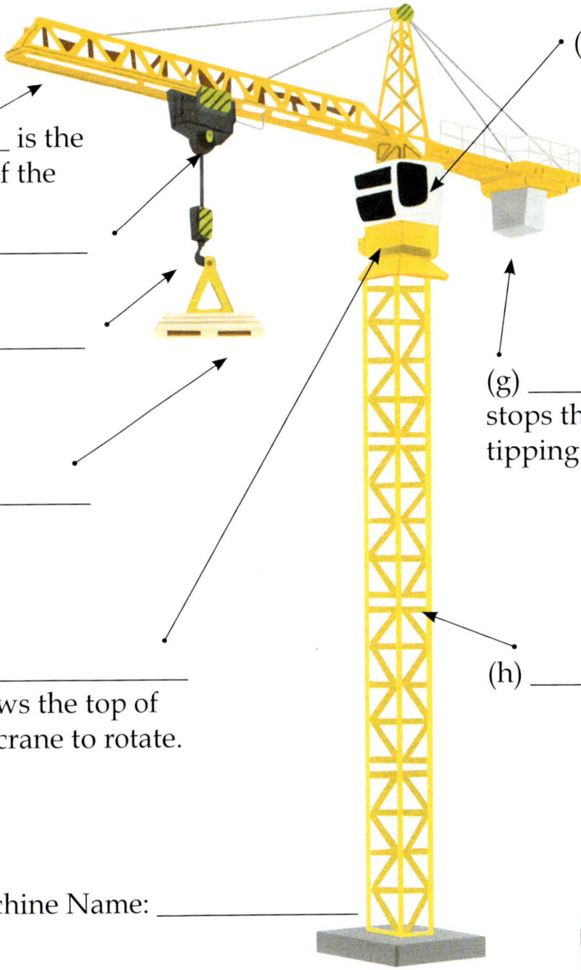

(a) ________ is the main arm of the crane.

(b) ________

(c) ________

(d) ________

(e) ____________ allows the top of the crane to rotate.

(f) ________

(g) __________. This stops the crane from tipping over.

(h) __________

Machine Name: ______________

GLOSSARY

Accurate	exact
Cargo	goods carried on a ship, aircraft, or motor vehicle
Cavity	an empty space within a solid object
Compass	an instrument containing a magnetised pointer which shows the direction
Concrete	a building material
Fossil fuel	a natural fuel formed in the geological past from the remains of living organisms
Frequency	the rate at which something occurs
Non-renewable	not capable of being replenished
Oxygen	a colourless, odourless gas and the life-supporting component of air
Potential	the possibility of something happening
Streamlined	design that presents very little resistance to a flow of air or water
Terrain	a stretch of land
Vibrate	move continuously and rapidly to and fro
Wobble	move unsteadily from side to side

ANSWERS

Page 28.

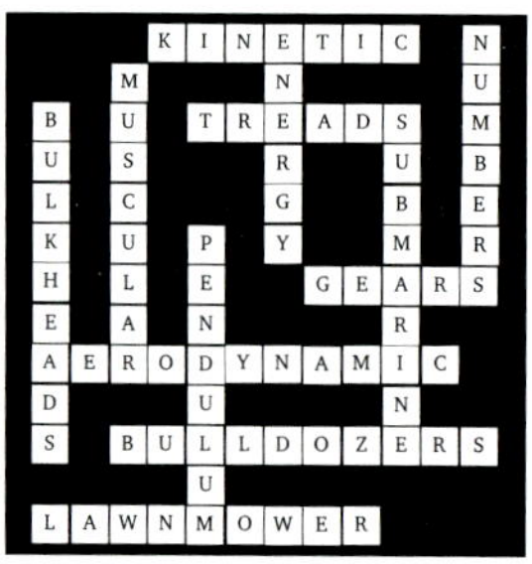

Page 29. 1. Tower Crane 2. Locks
3. Aeroplane 4. Ballpoint pen
5. Train 6. Digger

Page 30. 1.(c) 2. (a) 3. (c)
4.(b) 5.(b)

Page 31. Machine Name - Tower Crane
(a) Jib (b) Pulley (c) Hook (d) Load
(e) Slew Ring (f)Operator's cab
(g) Counterweight concrete (h) Tower